Europa 6 – The Beginning of the End

EUROPA 6 by Andy N and Nick Armbrister
© 2022. Andy N and Nick Armbrister. All rights reserved.
Authors: Andy N and Nick Armbrister

If you liked the book, then recommend your friends to download their own copy. Thank you very much for respecting the work of the author!

Thanks and Acknowledgements

Nick would like to dedicate this book to the writers in the world. Keep writing.

Cover photo by Nick Armbrister. Other photos by Nick Armbrister unless stated.

Dedicated to Vira Hyrych and Valeria Glodan and all of the others killed in Putin's senseless war. RIP…

Contents

Introduction -   7

Andy N   9

Nick Armbrister   39

Bios   87

Europa 6 – The Beginning of the End

Introduction

War is a funny business that goes without saying.

By funny, I don't mean comical (unless you count on how some invasions are planned afterwards in some ways) but in the sense of trying to work out why some things actually happen.

This could be a power trip, or some countries back in the 2000s who I won't name it became a war to get some oil. Whatever the reason, all things always lead to the same answer when countries attempt to take over violently neighbouring countries.

Death.

And Misery.

Often together.

And with mass death and slaughter following together hand in hand.

After the events that lead to Europa 5, it was never the plan for Europa 5 to follow with the speed it has followed barely a few months later when I was just finishing off my own segment for Europa 5 and I think Nick was in exactly the same situation as me and this happens.

It has to be said usually Nick and me usually take our time with these books and produce at a much slower pace than this book but times are very different at the moment.

Take 24 February 2022. This was a date one country which you will know got invaded in Eastern Europe by another in a major escalation of a War that began in 2014. If you research the facts, you will see this invasion caused Europe's fastest growing refugee crisis since the end of World War II with more 7.7 million people fleeding the country and a third of the population displaced.

Nick has mentioned with this invading country, the missile factories are working 3 shifts spread over 24 hours a day to produce more for the war effect and in the country under attack, I am constantly seeing film of their leader constantly asking for more help hidden away in a bunker while his people are dying on a daily basis.

It is not my place to say who is right or who is wrong here. I have my views as does Nick, but there is a lot of questions here which go unanswered why now for this invasion just after the world has being in the middle of Covid.

Why now just after the world got through the end of events of Afghanistan, and the chaos that has gripped America since Donald Trump left power?

What does the invading country really want from this invasion and how many more people will suffer because of it.

Sadly, the way things are starting to go – I suspect things will start to get worse before things get any better.

If there is a tomorrow to look forward for everybody.

Andy N
July 2022

Andy N
Airbrushing

I

Swapping matchsticks
he moved them
in-between the man's toes
before setting fire
searching for information
how to get across the border.

II

Never just because of war
you could count the bodies
Never just because of war
lined up all over the street
Never just because of war
one sided blanked in death.

III

After the bombing finished;

lost in despair

you described how your street

collapsed in seconds

killing nearly everybody

before the sun even rose.

IV

Sat there in a bunker you could

barely speak into Zoom account

let alone speak at an online poetry night

instead just letting your tears

carry your emotions

instead of a few frightened verses.

V

Mercenaries the leaked report said;
they were that desperate to win this war
10,000 criminals, outlaws, murderers
all were recruited from all kinds of sources
and pointed towards the villages to destroy
without mercy they came across.

VI

The attacks on the health centres
and the hospitals
were the most shocking;
destroying maternity wards and hospitals
their bombs silencing truth
as well as hope.

VII

And in the background

some countries stayed neutral

while others watched people bursting

onto news programmes

proclaiming 'They're lying to you'

leaving everybody more and more terrified.

VIII

43,800 signed up in the first five hours

to say come and live in England

43,800 held out their hands

to come and hide in their arms

43,800 and no doubt thousands more

making their own terrified choices.

IX

Playing Piano

over watching the carnage;

the silence in-between my notes

while composing

highlights the emotion

in my shock.

X

Could you blame her, the solicitor couldn't say

of course in a statement outside the court

when asked did he know where

the demonstrator at the State TV Station was

instead saying he had no address

unclear whether she had ran or being grabbed.

XI

The court appearance barely a few hours later

Was the most surprising almost like the news

before of her disappearance wasn't enough

to terrify people either further

but a warning they will control everything

before and during the actual case.

XII

And of course the longer it lasted

The worst the hunger and the darkness got

with hundreds left forgotten in cellars

afraid to step outside

in fear of the return of the airplanes

becoming rats instead of humans in days.

XIII

Escaping Justice
even her solicitor wasn't sure
whether she would be there
after 14 hours of interviewing
let alone what state
she would be in.

XIV

Looking downwards
her solicitor couldn't speak
when they they just fined her
leaving him thinking afterwards
if it hadn't hit the press
god knows what they would have done.

XV

'It won't be like the Syrian Civil War' The General proclaimed

at the press conference after another day of heavy fighting

'This won't go for eleven years with our forces'

clicking his fingers under the table in fear

full well knowing it very likely will carry on that long

no matter what he said unless peace could be found.

XVI

Vodka was the first thing to go of course

when sanctions began to kick in;

The space in the shelves in the supermarkets

left empty as a reminder

of what used to be there for people

before everything changed.

XVII

Temporary releasing control;
a famous ex footballer handed access
of his Instagram account to a doctor in the war
showing pregnant women and mothers
being moved into the basement of hospitals
highlighting their unbroken spirit to millions.

XVIII

Protestors met a superyacht
owned by a Billionaire close to the leader
as it tried to dock in Turkey
waving flags in protest of the country invaded
their rage carried across countries
unable to do anything but protest.

XIX

Unable to eat the billionaire complains
'I can't even pay to eat in a restaurant'
after his assets are frozen abroad from the war
when his links to the dictator are revealed
not thinking there are people living on sewer water
in the middle of the war zone.

XX

And even on a quiet day on the news
the focus by the press on the war
hovers but rarely moving away
turning the reports away briefly
with their cameras prepared to flick back
in the hope of more carnage.

XXI

Peace is another step closer the papers claim

only to then claim the refugee exodus

has hit four million

and is expected to keep rising

diluting the claims into dust

the truth into not even carefully thought lies.

XXII

Despite claiming after peace talks

they would cut back on the shelling

reports came from authorities of

35 artillery attacks in 24 hours on local towns

leaving everybody wondering if they called this

cutting back on artillery attacks.

XXIII

134,000 the decree declared new soldiers

would have be called up

barely days after proclaiming

the shelling would be eased off

almost like they were getting more ready

to replace who had being killed.

XXIV

And then there was the general

rumoured to have being run down

by some of his own men

sickened by the endless casualties

buried in shadows out of their sight

and the whispers off the endless media.

XXV

A quarter of the population
the papers reported;
barely six weeks into the war fled;
some sending their children to Poland
others hiding underground
hoping tomorrow they could go home.

XXVI

16,000 they claimed to have
shipped in from the Middle East
volunteering to come to serve them
to take the towns and cities
their knives like presidents money
their bullets like garbled prose.

XXVII

Stun Grenades witnesses claimed;

they threw Stun Grenades

into a peaceful protest of people

simply begging for food

almost like they knew if they didn't

what their generals would do it to them.

XXVIII

And a hundred miles away

soldiers pulled backwards

with crowds cheering briefly

before falling silently

unclear if others would be returning

to take their place the day after.

IXXX

Perhaps the most shocking

was children from the enemy

being used as human shields in conflict

with both sides stood there in shock

and their captains unable to shout

sickened to the core with their orders.

XXX

"We had thought invasions of other countries,

savage street fighting and atomic threats

were grim memories of a distant past,"

Pope Francis said upon revealing plans to visit

his elderly hands shaking with rage

wishing he could do more than just offer hope.

XXXI

57 people were found buried
in a mass grave;
some partially buried in the earth
jostled together in the darkness
almost like their killers
didn't think nobody would miss them.

XXXII

One mother cries on television
barely able to look at the camera
as she describes her son hiding bread;
afraid they'll soon run out of food
millions of others joining them in shock
without needing to answer on twitter.

XXXIII

The sanctions were working,

they claimed costing them 3.6 billion

from oil and gas sales in March

before then claiming machine gun like

it would will lead to food shortages

and spike migration in poorer countries.

XXXIV

We will not supply our products

and agricultural products to our enemies."

They stated in response to more firms

closing up their business and walking away,

their treats offering a number of alternative endings,

all trapped in wire nettings.

XXXV

Weeks and weeks

the satellite cameras claimed

the bodies were left strewn across

the quiet tree-lined street

bullet shells laid on the floor

next to severed fingers and hands.

XXXVI

That didn't happen the Minister claimed

while presented with the footage

upon getting quizzed by the press

how many more bodies was there

when the first

of the mass graves was found.

XXXVII

Away from the news for two days;

We may have missed the news

but those in the firing zone

would not have the opportunity

to step away from the carnage

or the constant bombings.

XXXVIII

The image of the ginger cat

sat there looking at the body

like a child looking at their parent

paying a silent tribune

wishing they could do more

as much as looking for their next dinner.

XXXIX

100 million worth of weapons our leader announced

after the bombing of refugees at a railway station

which left dozens cut to pieces and buried under rubble

were on the way to them to assist with their war;

still a chancer declaring what has being done is wrong

and losing his anger in landscapes of noisy silence.

XXXX

25 nights the farmer described taking the reporters

'I slept here in a half metre of space, I was sleeping standing up,

I tied myself to the railing here with my scarf so I wouldn't fall over'

His words split open across the basement

sharing space with the dead when nobody would dare more them,

their lives like a goldfish on the point of fracture.

XXXXI

Crying all night long

3,000 soldiers have being killed

in just over seven weeks

their president said

before looking downwards

they would be more to come.

XXXXII

And over in the invading country

after seven weeks they begin to ban leaders

from dozens of other countries

flying in for talks

instead threatening unpredictable consequences

if they keep supplying weapons.

XXXXIII

Fearing a Nuclear War

you begin to see the tins get less and less

in first your local supermarket

then the corner shop

and then hear your neighbour complaining

their shelf has collapsed.

XXXXIV

Fearing a Nuclear War

your Prime Minster denies the claim

in an interview saying it was unlikely

and then encouraged everybody

for Wine time Fridays

clearly more interest in drink than War.

XXXXIII

Get out by Easter Monday

they threatened to one City

or face mass slaughter

if they don't put down their weapons

streaking the nightmare into a roadmap

the air into a bitter taste of tension.

XXXXIV

And for those who fled to other countries

the government banned people

from trying being put them into caravans

without realising the refugees

would sleep anywhere, anywhere

but where they came from.

XXXXV

Leaving Easter

the breeze is making speech

as another building is flattered

and the United Nations stated

4,869,019 people have fled

and countless others have being killed.

XXXXVI

And into Day 55 after Easter,

the tension won't go away

following you across the river then the forests

with the leader under attack

hoping the American leader will visit

almost like it will help out.

XXXXVII

Months some reports claimed
some of the soldiers have being told
the war could go on
and the body count will keep rising
until there will be no land
or brothers to build the harvest.

XXXXVIII

And unless the war is finished soon
the same report claimed
both countries will be left close to starving
unless things change
and everybody can find peace
without the constant shelling and killings.

XXXXIX

What if the invasion failed
one of the TV reporters asked
months into the conflict
Would things return to the past
They finished looking ahead
knowing it was impossible.

XXXXX

And on the news a journalist
says he was beat repeatingly
for speaking out against them
'this was his re-education'
he said he was told
bringing peace no nearer

XXXXXI

'Almost every family
has lost somebody close'
One witness said
'Everything is lost for everyone'
bringing reality closer
repainting the airbrushing of history.

XXXXXII

Destroying generations
the body-count still rises
with no end in sight and blocks collapsing
with dozens crushed to death
and nobody allowed to help
Destroying generations.

Nick Armbrister

Quietness

i wanna hike monte cassino
i wanna hike the seelow heights
i wanna hear the roar of the guns
i wanna hear the wounded scream
i wanna hear the silence of history
i wanna feel a million deaths
i wanna hear all their stories

Glass Plates

Oh how his head was full of flies
Buzzing round this way and that
Like enemy bullets many times
In his 27 years of service
Vet means vet not for the pets
War veteran almost 3 decades
Serving his country multiple times
Mostly in the arsehole places
Those are hard to find on a map
For normal civvy people
Impossible for him to forget
The memories are bullets
Of blasts bombs death
Not left on the battlefield
Now in his head bad PTSD
Bad as in you weren't there
And will never ever get it
Not get a bullet like he did
The Allied vet with issues
He doesn't need tissues
Oh no his wounds are there
Not fixable in or out
Debilitating they call it
War flashbacks ignite him
Petrol burn anger immediate
Kill or be killed get in his way
Send him to the VA hospital
If they fail and he loses this war
He leaves there in a box
Finally joins his dead buddies

At eternal rest moment forever frozen
They gave their all just kids
Armed with guns and tanks
Part of him is missing
Shot out by enemy bullets
Still on that battlefield
One of many he saw
All unique all the same
Like a plate of glass he says
He lost himself again
The Canadian ex vet

Little crashes

STONE/KUROSAWA TARAC RIDGE
SUNNY 8 CASTLEFIELD MOOR
HELLCAT PILOTS CAPAS TARLAC
ON AND ON
RIP

Wirraway

Ting ting ting go the small bullets
Swat them away like mosquitoes
Little pretty named Australian warplane can't catch the big
Japanese seaplane so he screws the engine
And keeps distance like a South East Asian truck
The Wirraway pilot aims his twin little pop guns
And hoses the Nip mothertrucker down
Poor old Mavis seaplane gets hit
But keeps on flying along like an Isuzu truck
You need a Corsair or Hellcat to splash this
And so the frustrated Aussie Wirrwway went
Away way Wirraway back to his base
The stupid high command ordering us to be here
Used as fighter interceptor planes!
Put them in the cockpits see how they do
In these small low powered attack planes
And yes most of our brave pilots in their planes
Paid the price shot down damaged killed injured
But all wasn't as it seemed and it was this way
Decades later the Aussie Wirraway pilot
Met a real live Jap who shook his head and said No
I will not tell you what happened on that flight deck
Of our Mavis seaplane when you hosed it
One thousand rounds like mossies zing ping ding
Hitting damaging wounding killing us here
Rifle calibre rounds on target have an affect
I refuse to tell you what your bullets did...

From war records:

A notable interception from Rabaul took place on the 17th January 1941 when the CO of 24 Sqn, Sqn Ldr Lerew took off in a Wirraway from a dispersed strip at Kavieng in a hurry wearing only his shorts, with no parachute, goggles etc in pursuit of a Kawanishi `Mavis' flying boat which had just bombed his strip,......he reached 16,000 feet where his teeth were chattering due to the cold but he located the Mavis 8,000 feet below and dived to make a head on attack,......damaging the flying boat and killing two crew but the enemy aircraft was too fast for him and managed to pull away and head back to Truk. Many years later after the war the Australian and Japanese pilots of this action met up.

I wish mystery/what you all did sky events peace?/silly boys planes guns

Upper heights

also you need to hike here mt mataba
with your background you owe it to the soldiers dear hope
such death in such beauty
i dunno wot to say girl
i wish it was a fairy tale baby
if i take a million pretty gals like you there
maybe it will help fix wot men in war did there
this peak
fucking hell

Japanese Tunnel

The Japanese tunnel was hidden by grass
Look about and you wouldn't see it
How lovely is that untouched war site?
Local mountain man knows of it
Will show you this little secret
An entrance you have to crawl thru
It goes in part way and there's a turn
This is to stop blast and bullets
Harder to kill the Japs then
Hiding round a corner to get you
I want to see this site if it's ok
Not collapsed or unfindable
What is its story?

Bros

how did i find about on the bataan warplane crashes? ha a google search then i put an expedition together. we never found yankee pilot stone. rip bro. sorry i failed your brother wes who wanted answers on your location. i was simply too late. i wanna go up there again to look for yankee pilot stone. my dad is to blame. this thing i carry with me for the world war 2 pilots. all of them. i wish it wasn't so but of course i accept, selflessly...

Kurosawa

japan pilot kurosawa killed in action with usa pilot stone. rip. both are equal in death. tarac ridge bataan philippines. yes that is a bone. both were in a dog fight. both flew for their fucking lives. only the mother goddess and the dead pilots knew what happened that day feb 8 1942. fuck war.

Stone

curtiss p40 warhawk/kittyhawk/tomahawk crash with usa pilot stone. we looked for his remains. he is still mia missing in action. tarac ridge bataan philippines

GREEN PLEASANT LAND ENGLAND

my GREEN PLEASANT LAND ENGLAND. the cost of all this is unreal. yankee mustang pilot died here. not sunny 8 pilot. he went in over the hill. his wingman lost a wing tip lol. i only address what happen here with drink. lots of drink. i guess there are my opposites who feel the same at the peak in germany where five focke wulf 190s went in. it's simply surreal and cannot be written...

Mushroom Catastrophe

I used to think that all roads led to Poltava
I was wrong for all roads lead to death
I was in Ukraine in 2018 and saw myself
The cost of their sons killed by Russian fire
Brothers killing brothers all for Putin
He took Crimea then East Ukraine
By forming terror forces not under flag
It'll only get worse for them and us all
Ending in a mushroom catastrophe
All dead ash ghosts memories gone
Like the song 99 Red Balloons by Nena
She was right and we were wrong
To believe in peace for peace's sake
Only the year has changed
NATO expanded eastwards
Russia hated it 3 decades later acted
With plans in place to re-draw the map
NATO will not back down nor the USA
Only Satan will smile with glee
Watch the skies...

Ghost Live

The Russian ghosts shake their heads in dismay
For this generation now has a war in their area
They never learnt nothing or settled by dialog
All they do is shoot kill explode destroy
Its worst in the built up areas here it's total

Toppled building full of dead people
Makes good sniping and defensive positions
Give Russian troops a new Stalingrad
But in the Ukraine bleed the Red Army white
Make every town like this so they pay the price
They can have the open steppe there's nothing there
Hit their supply lines no shells or fuel all burnt

Give then a new Afghanistan here and now
That's if they don't pull back return to barracks
Give Putin the war he threatens so he loses
And is booted from power the failed dictator
Losing his wanted war with a million dead
They never learnt their lesson it's applied again
Watch the TV and you'll soon see

Boy And Girl

Russia and Ukraine are at it again
Just like a rowing couple so silly
And that was that is was all over before it began
They was given duff info and knew the truth
And saw it with their own eyes and skeward mind
Their version of events was different than his
Ukrainian and Russian both were opposite
Yet were oddly the same as shared things
They compare at opposite poles and feelings
They wanted certain things made many demands
The other side wanted the opposite
Neither agreed to meet in the middle
Russia was a girl Ukraine a boy
Both were at war after a lover's quarrel
Millions would die due to their stupidity
Blame the leaders blame the army blame
Or simply blame the world blame for it all
It was all over before it began
Except in our minds' eye

Time Come

The soldier looks very smart
In his new army uniform
With his toy plastic looking assault rifle
Slung diagonally across his chest
A cop playing a wannabe soldier
See how he is under fire when the Reds
Those dirty commy Reds open fire
On him after invading his homeland
Will he shoot and hit first or die?

Shall we send an enemy patrol to see?
How the soldier does under fire and stress
The cop now bumped up a job grade
Not just a small pistol an added rifle
None of this matter without training
And the will to fight to stop the Reds
Across the world in many nations
The time is approaching...

Game Over

There they lie all in a row
Not saying much just now
Due to being stone cold dead
Missing body parts and bits
This guy has a leg gone
His pal has no arm
The one opposite no head
Another lost eight ribs
All lost their lives sorely
If they could talk now
They'd have many words
Thoughts emotions to say
All agreeing on one thing
They are dead soldiers
Killed in the war
Game over now

Man Isle

From Russia with love ten thousand missiles
All for NATO the US Europe and Ukraine
Forged in battle ordered fired by Putin
New way to do things poor cold soldiers

Sent to battle warm them up!
Peace sells nobody's interested
Unless it's cut-price Vipers or stealth jets
Locked and loaded get you some blood
Neo Soviet Ivan style a few new scalps

Doesn't matter we weren't enemies
Pretending is fine as Putin does it
As he plays top dog woofing along
His ongoing Ukraine war after Syria
Where will be next the Isle of Man?

I

Neo Soviet sleeper cells lying in wait
Or just crossing the border at varied places
Troop checkpoints or a forest path
Or by HALO jump from a plane
Doing their job changing the landscape
Not chopping down trees
But assassinating those on the list
Culling the ones who were an issue
That Putin wanted dead out of the way

II

Ukraine belonged to Russia
So they acted doing their job
To make things easier
Ukraine was Russia
Russia was Ukraine
Outsiders don't get it
One Mother Russia
Always forever

Adventure Days

They say a cornered man will fight till the end
For simply has nothing to lose
Except his life when the cards are revealed
The dice is rolled balls to the wall kaput
You know what I mean no more examples
Need to be said but one final example
That of Ukraine in February 2022
Since late 2021 the nation has been
Threatened by Neo Soviet Russia
Surrounded on 3 sides by hostile land
The 4th side is water which they can own
NATO flew in Javelin and Stinger missiles
To kill tanks choppers and jets
The Ukrainians have enough bullets
Most made in Russia or the Soviet Union
To kill their fellow brothers who turned
On them in the worst case of cabin fever
That Europe has seen since Yugoslavia
And Marshall Tito's precious union died
This will be far worse than that
Could kill millions ruin Europe the world
Trigger World War 3 like a Tom Clancy book
Or a video game or heavy metal song or film
But this little escapade by Putin is real
He re-armed Russia and wants his empire back
He's part way there but millions will refuse
To be ruled from Moscow and be proxies again
Those days are gone except in his rabid mind

Soon his army must be used or go home
It is tiring and costs millions to be ready
The 200,000 Russian Red Army at readiness
Waiting for the order to invade their kin
Over the border brothers and sisters
Many with dual nationality and identity
But Ukraine is a sovereign nation
And will fight back as they've done since 14
When Putin the Dog annexed Crimea
And took East Ukraine which he still holds now
He wants the rest and for them to be his
Never ever join NATO and be European pals
Plus allied to the Yankees his worst nightmare
Ruining his dream the world their lives WHY???

Putin

They started it let the cat out of the bag
It's in a ferocious mood after being confined
Imagine how you'd feel kept in a tied-up sack
Now the feral cat wants revenge and gets it
Rampaging this way and that killing eating
Quenching its blood lust till spent
Not stopping till the job is done
And the cat is at peace
No longer prodded poked kicked
Ridiculed laughed at in a sack
She's free now and will remain so
Even if it means doing what she does
With claws and teeth and other things
Keep an eye out for her approaching
Only the cat knows whose next

Modified Bombs

Her eye was acting up but that was fine
For she had a second one to use
This was just fine like her warplane
It had two engines but number one engine
This was like her eye acting up too
No need to worry for Eagle 2 jets are good
Made with system redundancy like her
An ability to function with degraded systems
Right now she was on the way to Moscow
To drop some iron bombs on Putin
A personal gift from a gal who was bad
Real bad ass half Yank half what?
That last bit was unknown but what was
Known was that she would soon be dead
Along with the Neo Soviet leader
Those iron bombs were special
She'd personally modified the warheads
A new historical dawn was coming...

Rabid Putin

The crazed cliché of Putin went mad
And invaded Ukraine from four sides
Three on land and one by sea

Using choppers jets tanks
Missiles bombs rockets guns
Killing till killing was done
Getting killed in return by their bros

Who defended their land
Never turned their backs
Fought and died for Ukraine
Splashed several enemy aircraft

As Putin threatened NATO
With nuclear war but hey
It goes both ways
So smokes the mushroom clouds
In a future chapter of this Putin play book

The Baltic republics will be next
Then Poland and others
Putin will lose but so will we
Except the Devil so many dead...

Again blistering/detonations Ukraine now/Russia falls later

Dancing Day

There is a party in the park will you go the
Theme is military so bring a toy weapon
We will play at war it will be so much fun
You can be Russia I will be NATO
The others Red China North Korea etc
So we all get a really good battle war
Just a game at our little party in the park
Do come along it will be a day to remember

Second Kennel

So the rabid dog left his kennel to go steal another kennel
This kennel belonged to a relative and was quite nice
But it was a bit smaller and not as well equipped
Still the dog wanted it and went for it
Trying to steal it take it use abuse it
Why have one kennel when you can have two?
Acquired by other means no matter what method
The dog is crazy but in his mind all is fine normal the world

It turns and he tells a story as he sees it
All things rabid not quite right up there
They say command is the loneliest place
Even God gets lonely so he made Satan
Even if enemies God aint alone there

Unlike the dog giving orders do this and that
Go get my second kennel even if it breaks
I want that kennel don't let them keep it
It must belong to me!

Missile Ways

What's up the sky and the Russian planes?
Before they're splashed by Stinger missiles
Whoosh! Missile away go go go kill a jet
Or chopper bring it down in the water
Let the crew freeze or drown
Some burn alive or get killed in the crash
How dare they invade Ukraine!
Teach them all a lesson forever
Some things not to be forgotten
Like Duncan in Dune 2021 die superbly
Never surrender no matter what
This is how Ukraine is now
No matter what happens
Ukraine wins Russia loses
Splashed enemy aircraft
Dead aircrew Putin kaput

Tupolev 141 Drone

Those old drones and planes and choppers all sat there just waiting to fly to war. Polish the metal fuel them up kick the tires away they go. No crew just needed just a memory of flight. Something part of their fabric like their wings or engine. A thing part spirit part elemental that exists beyond human comprehension though we built the machines.

Now they're ready to go almost a race of beings from elsewhere. Maybe an alien intelligence possessed them to make them fly. Let them get even with the Russian soldiers and leaders. For violating Ukraine and other areas out of their realm.

Of course they're just machines and vehicles. Not alive or able to fly alone. But why are their parking bays and taxi strips and museum display areas now empty? Where did the drones choppers and planes go? Of to Russia to fight bomb kill ram obliterate them till victory is here for the good guys.

More Stupidity

Putin sent in his air force to further bomb Ukraine
Hitting Dnipro for the first time killing and wounding more
My friend lives there and I'm glad he's ok
He's got both Ukrainian and Russian citizenship
This war is like him fighting himself
Or America and Canada going at it
The worst exercise in stupidity anywhere
All thanks to Putin the rabid dog
I wonder how many Russians living in Ukraine
Have been killed by his little war?
Plus his own soldiers blown to bits
Yankee missiles work very well
Ask the Russian pilots and tankers
Like everyone else I ask when it will end

All Putin's Fault

The man cries
No more wife
No more child
No more family
No more home
No more Ukraine
No more happiness
Huge bomb craters
All Putin's fault

Ongoing

The pretty lady screams
KILL ME NOW!!!
Putin's bombs just murdered her baby
What life will the young mum have now?
In a shattered country war death hate killing
The bastard waited decades for this

And acted not caring the cost
Of Russia's neighbouring nation
Plus thousands of dead Russian soldiers
Let the traumatised lady be an example
Of what it's like to be in Putin's war

Like the husband's family also killed
By Putin's mortar bombs while waiting
To flee their devastated homeland
Remember them all make him pay
For every single death and injury
And ruined town and city...

By Sixes

With this book we have to make a difference
The weight of worry and seriousness is huge
This has not happened before not this way
And very soon all things could happen
They try to control it but can they?
How do you control so many soldiers?
Along with the other shooters
Planes ships launchers tanks and more
Myself I've never felt this way
Except briefly in the early 80s
The world moved on in most ways
But not in Putin's head for him
He alone wants his empire back
And will ruin the world to get it
This is why we all must not fail
And stop him from winning
Even if the unthinkable happens
It has already started the walk
Sleep walking to Armageddon
NATO and Russia and the rest
This is really it...

Vivid Orange

Sky black burnt like sack cloth by the fires
Endless fires vivid orange flames
Always orange as is the screams
Now invisible for they are dead
Bodies black ash blown about
Wind whipped up by the flames
Orange wind this way and that
Like the war win lose win lose
On and on till it simply ended
All dead nobody left to fight
Pull the trigger drop the bomb
Only orange remains so vivid
Like the old sports cars burnt orange
Part of the new world free of humans
Putin went mad NATO stopped him
The rest joined in so the world ceased
Just orange fires burning the skies
Little is now here from before

20 Cents

The guy gave the war concern 20 cents
This was enough to buy ten bullets
Which would kill ten enemy soldiers
If fired accurately by a good soldier
He'd give more if he could afford it
But he was jobless and skint
20 cents was all he could afford
Bread and coffee cost money
Even if cheaper thru the VA
His benefits were little not enough
So he just gave 20 cents
To the war collection team
When they knocked on his door
It brought back memories
Vietnam and Central America
Plus other deniable places
Still alive in his head
He didn't like Russians
So 20 cents was fine
The cost of ten bullets
For a competent soldier
He prayed they wouldn't miss
Once he was a soldier
With many good kills
All of them Russians...

In Silence

The English ex SAS Special Forces member went to the Ukraine to fight. He travelled light and took just a small back pack and a head full of skills. A gun was a gun and a bayonet a bayonet. He was trained to use most things as weapon especially military articles.

He decided to go to the Ukraine after the Russians invaded proper in early 2022. The Ukrainian Army took him to a holding facility where they vetted him. This took three days. Included was basic close combat skills and weapons use.

He excelled and was given a job, being sent to a forward artillery position with a dozen other foreign troops to protect it. The SAS man was in charge and most men and the single girl spoke English. All understood military commands and signals. All were veterans from either conscript or professional armies.

Each was here for their own reasons and all disliked either what Russia had done or Russians themselves. The English SAS member had killed several Muslim terrorists from Daesh and al Qaeda in Iraq and Afghanistan. Now he looked forward to fighting and killing some Russians, officers if possible. After being in the Ukraine six days he was on the front line leading his first patrol. This was better than being a bouncer in a Manchester night club!

The SAS guy ordered his men to only use bayonets as they silently crept to a Russian fox hole a mile away. He wanted blood and the rush of combat, of killing. There was the trench and a single sentry, asleep. He would knife him himself. Then his squad would murder the rest and take back any weapons, maps or documents. He spoke four languages including Russian. Any Intel was good for his bosses though. Here we go! There's the sleeping sentry. Gently now, he must die in silence…

Radioactive

The goth boy was beautiful like what Liz Hand wrote
In her book The Glimmering he was so perfect
In his black satin shirt open to the chest and more
Showing his varied metal chains and necklaces
One had a pendant on another a small padlock
I wondered what they mean? Only he knew
He wore a black mask against the CCP Virus
Pulled down below his nose almost stylish
His black shoulder bag had BLACK written on it
In white writing to emphasize the point
With hard core black Doc ankle boots
The only thing missing was a music t shirt
This would spoil the effect of how perfect he was
He was from Mariupol and wanted to take me out
To the theatre to see some culture and art
His city by the sea was like Odessa
Full of cultured people like him and sculpture
Art in all ways that you have to see live feel
But that was impossible now for they were gone
All dead by the enemy Russian shelling
I cried and drank and talked to his ghost
And listened to him describe what we'd do
When we went out to the theatre
And to a goth club later to see band
His sister was Russian a lovely gal
I'd gotten her pregnant and we were married
She'd died early on in Kiev with our kids
Now our bro was gone too as was our city
Soon the world would follow all of it
Do not remember us or the goth boy
We are just dust in the wind invisible
Radioactive like the rest of you...

Different War

The Russian forces do not care for their pilots
In their advanced warplanes and choppers
They send them in again and again but not a thousand
Just enough to lose a few and expend Ukrainian missiles
Will the planes and pilots run out before the missiles?
A war of attrition that's different than others
Yet the fighting and killing is the same so it's similar
Russia's first peer on peer war with a smaller equal
Brothers fighting their own in a vicious fight
Clichés apply both old and newly made ones
Missiles versus jets nothing new the way it's done
Sending them day after day a hundred splashed
Russia will lose the battle who will win the war
Allied missiles do the killing Stinger Javelin NGLAW
Russia will remember we will remember Russia
Or Putin for this is his war his alone
He murdered his soldiers pilots
And Ukrainians...

Shout of 'Air!' comes in/Ukrainian pilot flies/one month of defence

More Crimes

People fleeing their shelled flaming town
Inhabitants no more Russian shells death
Driving the road a car full of their lives
Possessions priceless burning homes

Shattered shops ended lives busted up
Blown apart thousands dead mass graves
One chance only to escape their old homes
Not to be for there's Russian tanks!

They fire their machine guns
Hitting the cars wounding killing
A couple of cars U turn and flee
Several are unlucky hit burn stop

Gunfire screams explosions curses
Death bodies cars scenes stories
Will be later shown to the world
This is what the Russians still do

Killing innocent civilians in their cars
Not just in the city of Mariupol
More war crimes levelled on Putin
Added to the list crimes names of the dead
We all ask when and how will this end?

Bucha

So it happened again dozens of civilians murdered in cold blood
Killed in the hundreds by Russian forces or their allies
A new name is now known us all to symbolize a war crime

I'll let you judge if the events at Bucha are genocide or not
People walking or cycling down the street shot dead
More killed in houses tortured to death in basements

Unwanted bodies dumped in a big mass grave Nazi style
The Nazis did this in Ukraine in World War 2 old history
Repeated in 2022 by Putin's failing war machine

The casualties of war are always civilians it continues
First the war needs to be won by Ukraine then justice
This will be achieved an even harder battle to win

Get Putin and those responsible in the dock
Make sure this does not happen again
The world has said enough!

Very Nice

See her there
Hot tight butt
Nice small boobs
Long cool legs
Sweet seductive smile
Freshly painted nails
No make up
Mid length hair
Well used rifle
Shiny pointed bullets
Sharpened silver bayonet
Green army uniform
Yellow blue flag
Innocent Ukraine gal
Killing Russian troops
Defending her land
Gal's only unit
Do not forget
What happened here

Deciding

What to do today decisions to be made
Where to go what to wear who to see
Imagine if in the Ukraine what to do
Defend your sacred land till the end
Which Russian soldier to kill
How will you kill him?
Decisions decisions
What to do today
Which soldier dies?

Never Again?

Old Mariupol lady
Hid underground from Nazis
Russians killed her now

Old Mariupol lady
Hid underground from Nazis
Russians killed her now

Junk Bucket

In with the fishes bottom of the seabed
Russia's fine warship rusting junk bucket
Nothing but scrap metal decaying systems
Hit and sunk by Ukrainian missiles
Copied form Soviet ones do the job
Exocet style ask the Brits they know
What it's like to lose a ship in war
More will follow nothing floating
All being nice not war but hey
This is a book film video game
The story Tom Clancy should've written
With a happy ending in fiction
The real world is unforgiving
Abruptly real sunk ship the crew?
Russian Putin's lies there's no issue
Our ship is fine in port not sunk
Till even he realizes this is real
Neptunes got the Moskva kaput
Which junk bucket is next
Their coal powered carrier?

Arrows Up

Launched over Ukraine
Killing Ukrainians stone cold dead
Arrows down in Russia
Killing Russians burnt hot
Aint karma a bitch!

Little gals million tall

listening to 80s/new wave/goth/alternative/synth pop band BERLIN album VOYEUR and writing anti war story influenced by 3 gals. all 3 are very important in what they stand for. my words/views cannot fully state that or how i feel on multiple things. 2 of the gals are fine. 1 is ukrainian and is not ok. she was murdered by incoming russian fire. as were others. im doing a bit of writing, a script. this is my 1st script. a story told only in words. of course it will be dedicated to all 3 gals who inspired this dark art by lil writer activist me. but the gal who was stolen from here and another gal who is equally important, its for them. as a friend said to me today: 'he wishes they were both still alive...' so do i. rip. unconditional love always. i, we, will never ever forget. FUCK PUTIN and his war. i hope you ar ehappy with half your 120k army suffering sixty thousand casualties. karma is a bitch. you will learn this \m/

Will you use nukes?/we will publish our book when/peace falls down, ashes?

Nick Armbrister

Hi, my name is Nick Armbrister. I'm from Manchester, England. I've been writing since April 1996 and published since Nov 96. Very much part of the late 90s 'small press' writing scene, published in mags, 'zines, anthologies and later in the 00s, online and in my own books. I've worked for an American publisher before but left due to editing issues. Self published a hundred books under Nick Armbrister and my pen name Jimmy Boom Semtex. My variety of work is huge. I've written with a wide variety of poets/authors. Love to be creative, like hiking and high ground and also love tattoos and aeroplanes. My books are on the usual sites and stores.

https://nickgoth555.wixsite.com/website

https://jimmyboomsemtex.blogspot.com/

*

Andy N

Andy N is the author of six full length poetry collections, the most being 'Haiku of Life' and numerous split poetry books, mostly with his wife Amanda Nicholson and long-standing friend Nick Armbrister.

H is co-runs Chorlton Cum Hardy (Manchester, UK)'s always welcoming spoken word open mic night 'Speak Easy'.

He is the host / co-host of Podcasts such as Spoken Label, Reading in Bed and Storytime with Andy & Amanda and does ambient music under the name of Ocean in a Bottle.

His website is: http://onewriterandhispc.blogspot.com/

www.ingramcontent.com/pod-product-compliance
Lightning Source LLC
Chambersburg PA
CBHW080721120726
48001CB00010B/3100